Work

BY KATHY THORNBOROUGH • ILLUSTRATIONS BY KATHLEEN PETELINSEK

The Child's World®

PUBLISHED by The Child's World®
1980 Lookout Drive • Mankato, MN 56003-1705
800-599-READ • www.childsworld.com

ACKNOWLEDGMENTS
The Child's World®: Mary Berendes, Publishing Director
The Design Lab: Design
Jody Jensen Shaffer: Editing

PHOTO CREDITS
© Andresr/Shutterstock.com: 3; andresrimaging/iStock.com:
19; Digital Storm/Shutterstock.com: back cover, 21; eurobanks/
iStock.com: 20; GeorgeDolgikh/iStock.com: 18; geotrac/iStock.
com: 17; lsantilli/Shutterstock.com: 5; Jaimie Duplass/Shutterstock.
com: back cover, 6; leungchopan/Shutterstock.com: 7; Lisa F.
Young:Shutterstock.com: cover, 1, 13; Ljupco/iStock.com: 22;
IuriiSokolov/iStock.com: 16; monkeybusinessimages/iStock.com:
9, 14; omgimages/iStock.com: 4; StefanoLunardi/iStock.com: 23;
StockDisc 10; stockyimages/Shutterstock.com: 15; Tyler Olson/
Shutterstock.com: 8, 12; videodet/iStock.com: 11

ISBN 9781626873254
LCCN 2014934479

PRINTED in the United States of America
Mankato, MN
July, 2014
PA02216

A SPECIAL THANKS TO OUR ADVISERS:

As a member of a deaf family that spans four generations, Kim Bianco Majeri lives, works, and plays amongst the deaf community.

Carmine L. Vozzolo is an educator of children who are deaf and hard of hearing, as well as their families.

NOTE TO PARENTS AND EDUCATORS:

The understanding of any language begins with the acquisition of vocabulary, whether the language is spoken or manual. The books in the Talking Hands series provide readers, both young and old, with a first introduction to basic American Sign Language signs. Combining close photocues and simple, but detailed, line illustrations, children and adults alike can begin the process of learning American Sign Language. Let these books be an introduction to the world of American Sign Language. Most languages have regional dialects and multiple ways of expressing the same thought. This is also true for sign language. We have attempted to use the most common version of the signs for the words in this series. As with any language, the best way to learn is to be taught in person by a frequent user. It is our hope that this series will pique your interest in sign language.

Pilots fly everything from jets to helicopters.

Pilot

Bend your middle and ring fingers. "Fly" your hand foward. Then face your palms together and move downward.

3

Teacher

Move your hands outward,
away from your forehead.
Then face your palms together
and move downward.

Teachers must know
how to do many
things at once.

Carpenter

Carpenters know how to build and fix many types of wood and plastic.

Slide your right fist over your left palm. Then face your palms together and move downward.

Referee

Curl your index and middle fingers. Tap your mouth twice.

Referees must be able to stop arguments peacefully.

Doctor

Your right hand taps your left wrist twice.

Doctors must go to school for many years.

Nurse

Your right hand makes the letter "N" and taps your left wrist twice.

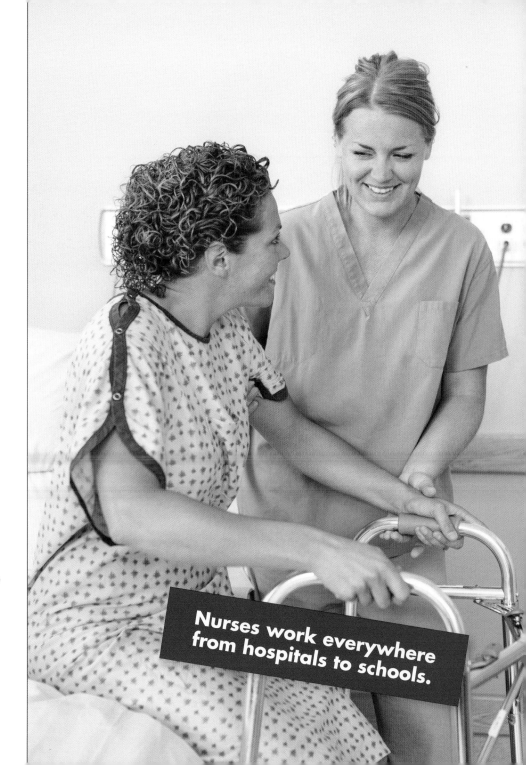

Nurses work everywhere from hospitals to schools.

Principal

Principals must have good leadership skills.

Make the letter "P" with your right hand. Circle around and touch the back of your left hand.

9

Painter

Move your right hand up and down against your left hand as if you were using a paintbrush. Then face your palms together and move downward.

10

Painters work on small houses and big buildings.

Soldiers must be patient and brave.

Soldier

Both of your hands make the letter "A." Your right hand taps your chest twice while your left hand taps your ribs twice.

Librarian

Make the "L" shape.
Circle around clockwise.
Sometimes this sign finishes
by facing your palms together
and moving downward.

Librarians must
love books
and reading.

Police Officer

Your right hand makes the letter "C" and taps your upper left chest like a police badge.

Police officers sometimes work very long hours.

Cashier

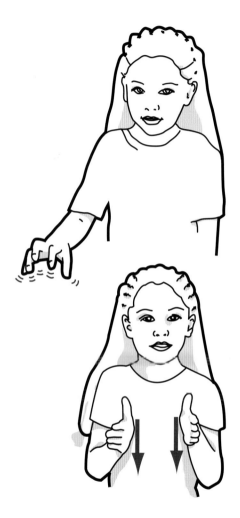

Wiggle your fingers as if you are using a cash register. Then face your palms together and move downward.

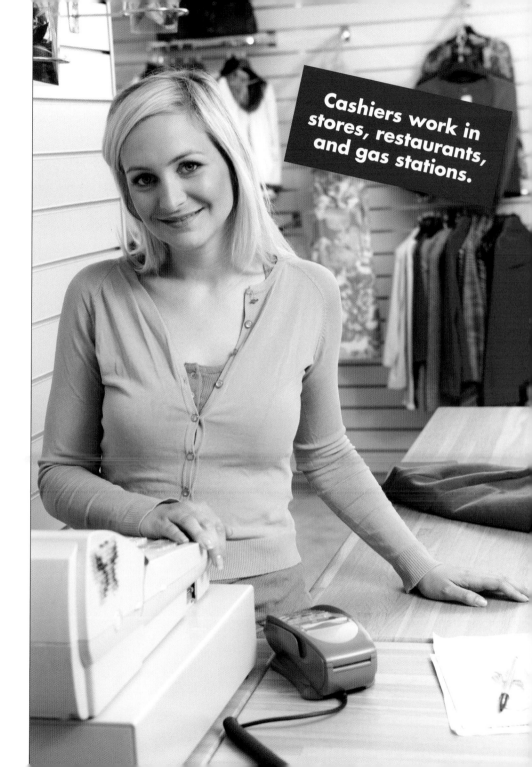

Cashiers work in stores, restaurants, and gas stations.

Cooks often go to special schools to learn their job.

Cook

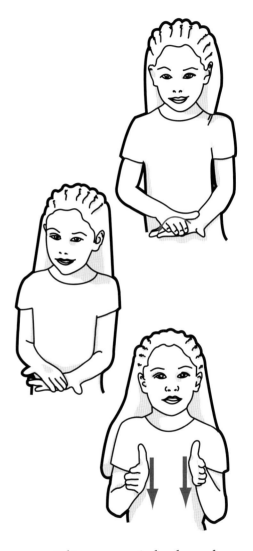

Flip your right hand
from palm-down to palm-up.
Then face your palms together
and move downward. **15**

Lawyer

Make the letter "L." Bump your fist against your flat left hand twice. Then face your palms together and move downward.

16

Lawyers must be good at speaking and writing.

Judge

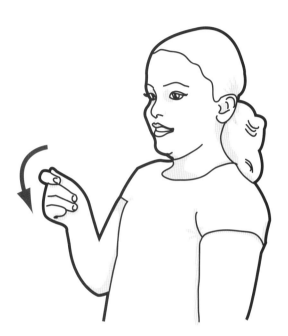

Pretend you are banging a gavel.

A judge must be a good listener. He or she must be patient, too.

17

Artist

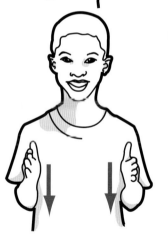

Make the letter "I" and move your pinky in a squiggly line down your left hand. Then face your palms together and move downward.

Artists work with everything from pencils and crayons to paint and plaster.

Actor

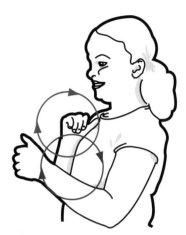

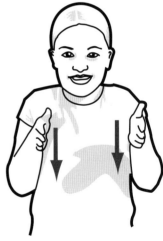

Make the letter "A" with both hands
and rotate in front of your chest.
Your thumbs brush your chest as
they go by. Then face your
palms together and move downward.

19

Coach

Your right hand makes the letter "C" and taps your right shoulder twice.

Some coaches volunteer. Others coach as their job.

Firefighter

Your flat right hand
taps your forehead twice.

Firefighters must know how to stay calm in emergencies.

Dancer

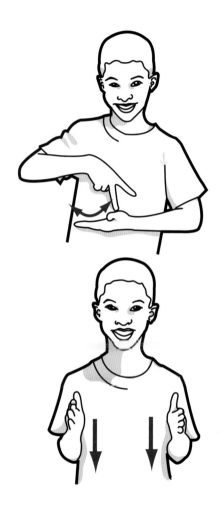

Make the letter "V" and swing back and forth over your left hand. Then face your palms together and move downward.

Dancers must be healthy and strong.

Farmer

Some farmers work on small farms. Others work for big companies.

Your open right hand moves from the left side of your chin to the right side. Then face your palms together and move downward.

23

A SPECIAL THANK YOU!

A special thank you to our models from the Program for Children Who are Deaf and Hard of Hearing at the Alexander Graham Bell Elementary School in Chicago, Illinois.

Alina's favorite things to do are art, soccer, and swimming. DJ is her brother!

Dareous likes football. His favorite team is the Detroit Lions. He also likes to play video games.

Darionna likes the swings and merry-go-round on the playground. She also loves art.

DJ loves playing the harmonica and video games. Alina is his sister!

Jasmine likes writing and math in school. She also loves to swim.

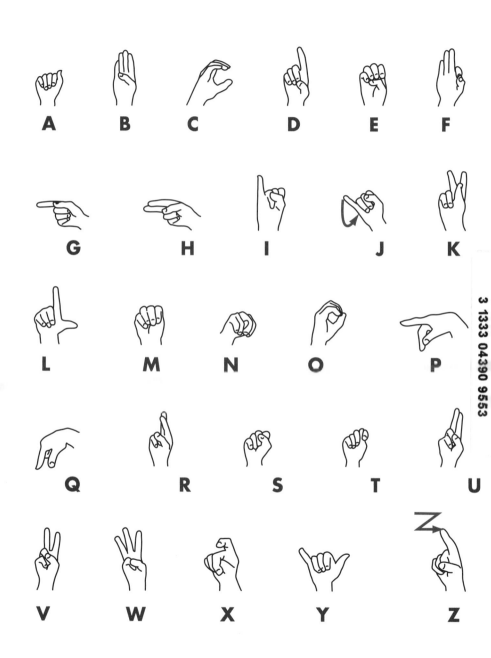